THE POETRY CORNER

JOEL WASHINGTON ATTERBERRY

The Poetry Corner
Copyrighted © 2020 Library of Congress
Published by: Joel Washington Atterberry
ISBN: 978-1-7352952-9-9
Contact Information
Email: kingatterberry7@gmail.com
Facebook: Joel Washington Atterberry
Instagram: king_atterberry7
Instagram: mentallity9

ACKNOWLEDGEMENTS

This book I dedicate to my cousin Quinten Ford, administrator of the Let's Talk group on Facebook. Thank you for the window of opportunity in providing me with an avenue for bringing THE POETRY CORNER show to life. We have started from the bottom with Season 1 and have entered a Season 2. May we voyage into future seasons and episodes, Cuzzo.

To my Uncle Destin Atterberry, who I love as if he were my brother, thank you for the lyrical consultation on my writings. Without your advice, I wouldn't have manifested the barz the way they are. Thank you, Uncle.

LET US BEGIN

THE POETRY CORNER

INTRODUCTION

Hello everyone, I am the author and the poet
Mr. Joel Washington Atterberry.

While spending time each week, normally on a
Tuesday, I host a poetry slam on facebook called
THE POETRY CORNER,
along with producer of the LET's TALK show,
Mr.Quentin Ford.

I invite guests to appear and recite their material
on the episodes of the show.
During my time of breaking ground with the show,
I have noticed my elevation point has marveled
into a new wave of writing.
I personally feel like I am one of the super-heroes
of spoken word poetry.
My quest for success has not ended. Along my
journey, I will use all of the tools within my skill
set to make it to the goal line.
There is much more work to be done.
So as you get to know me through my writings
here, let me re-introduce myself I am:

MR. JOEL WASHINGTON ATTERBERRY

TABLE OF CONTENTS

All for allure

When we chillin at the crib nothing strange to us.

Foundation of love with comfortable trust.

Sitting on the couch where our hands just touch.

Kissing so much because of time we make up.

Working so hard while the clock moves slow.

Enjoying our growth at a nice tempo.

All that matters in this world what we give to one another.

Making sure we capture moments, so our bond doesn't suffer.

Connecting our power so we shower with affection.

Praying on the blessings that we both been requesting.

Good enough feelings keeping our drive high and alive.

Seen enough to survive through my eyes from the sky.

Come on!!

When I spit pain with flames this is for all of yawl.

Go grab your six fifty extra strength Tylenol.

Piss and shit in your draws my guerilla tactics.

Tear hooks off your tracks list my lyrical practice.

Is to get bizzy who with me crowd around the underdog.

Exercise my law it's the words I keep raw.

Place seeds of doubt killing your mental focus.

Writing so explosive juicing off in high dosage.

Build on ciphers with enlightenment and righteousness.

Open doors with the greatest of my requirements.

Beginning of never-ending steady winning your mind spinning.

This is what I'm sending to those waiting your time pending.

building

Manifest no rest who the best still gets fresh kill the vet holds my breath say less open quest.

Knowledge wisdom understanding through the gods I'm on a start.

May we all embark inside the light from out the dark.

Different waves hitting shores getting more watch us score.

Step through halls marking floors enter doors watching walls.

From what I see and saw before many dynamics on the planet.

No longer is gigantic the ills of being frantic.

Only havoc is my thoughts posted up for eyes to see.

Point across inner force manifest my own degrees.

Jump out a window on an instrumental made by my fam.

It's THE MAN BEHIND THE HAND doing what haters can't.

I'm on first

Turn my back on those that want to look at me sideways.

Two days after Friday's my points bring tidal waves.

Never trust fools that be new take them to school.

Kings do what they do Staying away from shark pools.

I'm on land standing with my arms folded across chest.

Sporting a family crest embedded on a side, left.

When I was here before I didn't complete my task.

Had to step on different tracks that lead to better paths.

Walk through many places with the mindset of a god.

Here's a fifty-two pick up go ahead choose your cards.

Body of a Voltron spirited with five lions.

It's a Leo around the people august 1st I stay rising.

I will survive!!

There is a difference between what we see and what we know.

Learning from older folks about our own culture code.

Watch the badged beast when they opposite of peace.

No longer want to greet only beat to make us weak.

This time we struggle trying to keep our strength in muscle.

Keep our love for one another when we huddle and not tussle.

Lives matter cameras capture the brutality on us.

Who do you trust not the bluff of uniformed after us?

Keeping our mouths shut it's not a win win situation.

Nowadays we face illegal accusations some be hating.

The color of my skin or the confidence of my dignity.

My pride will stay alive even if my spirit cry and die.

Let's bring it back (hip-hop)

In the beginning they was winning and blending inside they living.

I drink snake venom and send them back to Hell's Kitchen.

Unaffected by the heat that's irrelevant come and visit.

Lock up your wizard with a lyrical blizzard watch how I spit it.

This time it's different got my studies from my old self.

Penning my own shit, I'm bringing bars back to health.

Teamed up with the razors and shank down the haters.

Still familiar with them pagers if my cell phone lose data.

Process this, reboot your system, redo your model.

Writing without a bottle while I'm reading a conscious novel.

I'm marvel and dc fight against the oldest rivals.

My writing become recitals like preachers with open bibles.

After all

Dark matter enters the flesh to possess.

Cross on my arm not my neck to protect.

Some hold they lives in another man's hands.

King never a fan only fam you understand.

The wise survive killing lies with paper flies.

Don't underestimate the guy with arms high.

Prayers upon the soldiers of this universal war.

Next time I do a tour, clear auras within my chores.

Speak amongst elites with no offset heartbeat.

Practice what I preach go underground for a week.

Maybe go down south find myself a Georgia peach.

Elevate in the heat while I rise on two degrees.

Pardon me excuse you

When I tap into the stream of music I start writing.

Thought waves are active my broadband is heightened.

Levels are increased when I release a form of speech.

Just know I'm bringing heat that have you moving your feet.

Step into the mind of a rhyme fanatic soldier.

I remember the god told that me all facts are solar.

Each one teaches one meet one and greet one.

Seek one and peep one the study hall is eastern.

Best of all the science and mathematics trump.

Not your president what's relevant you stay away from.

Ignorant behavior of media and the newspapers.

This is a new edition that I promote now than later.

Basic

Sitting between her legs getting my hair combed and braided.

New occasion waiting for **THE GUARD** that stay patient.

Power off a shower get dressed dip and chill out.

There's a party at a house where they want a different clout.

Beer kegs and food many people crowded around.

Even dancing to some sounds that other cultures found.

Mixed conversations while drinks are poured and passed.

Somebody in a group kindly asked where is the stash.

Stating we need plants just to enhance this gathering.

I'm time managing due to traveling while I am capturing.

Moments within minutes and seconds making connections.

Sweet honeys moving to the music with nice affection.

here we go

aye she taste like candy my nickname cameo.

make a guest appearance in her life my story untold.

walk a path real bright but she loves when I'm in flight.

I can travel destinations just meet me off the pike.

hands touch her body strong and soft no doubt.

fingers touch her lips because she knows what I'm about.

kiss the clouds for heaven's sake asking god to hold me down.

I'm the new dude in town besides, I just hit the ground.

she is showing me around, introducing me as L.

we are hanging out talking and laughing many stories to tell.

I'm fascinated by the area multi environment.

it getting late I'm wondering where the hell the time went

but I got other plans to take photos out at night.

caress the moon with my eyes oh yeah, I'm feeling right.

it's all about compassion caring and being cool.

let's see how I can move without a point to prove.

whether philly, dc, Baltimore or new yiddy.

this is just a poem to have them all say REALLY!

List one moving

Check your morning if your yawning don't be sleeping while awake.

In your lower power state protect your base and be safe.

Inside your vessel there's a true sea of life steady moving.

While you are choosing what you are doing

be-careful who you fooling.

Today's events may be dense just keep common sense.

Got to treat it like dirty laundry that's ready for wash and rinse.

When it's dry you realize the broken ribbon in the sky.

Hope and faith are still alive, got to survive the hidden lie.

Bring back the ciphers, group talks and lectures.

As a youth I learned from street corner teachers and professors.

Facts of each one teaches one speak to some help them.

Provide all with real gems feed they equilibrium.

Time after time

Before you saw the guard step into another chamber.

Excuse the early anger as I write and scribe a banger.

Forget verses you heard when I was nothing on the list.

I achieved a certain gift and started rhyming from the mist.

Give the pre world a kiss from the air before the evil.

Become deceitful killing the people contact the weasels.

Hold brands on land turn sands to dams free hands.

Comprehend the diagram when it's drawn witness a man.

Studies of liabilities trained inside facilities.

Moving with agility expressing grades of humility.

Resurrect the spark of real hearts in dark arks.

No twos what's due only renewed I'm checking charts.

Lyrical medicine

This is my P-nice dedication saluting an older mentor.

Rise of a protege that moved away to the shore.

All lessons from books that I explored and gained insight.

Helped the man behind the hands to write and take flight.

Minds thinking alike as the years were passing by.

Although my guardian angel was my eyes through the sky.

Elder named to me studied the world off what I seen.

From my brother became a music feign with a dream.

Tapes and CDs were memories of him and me.

Same house living as a youth since fourteen thirty.

Blessed to have a brother who was skilled as a professor.

Blood thicker than water raised by South Carolina & Georgia.

Must be the season

Woke up from sleeping it's a comic book weekend.

Superhero my way into the thoughts of those reaching.

To grab and hold playing a role to save civilians.

Much work to be done on the planet too many killings.

There's death upon my race of people still struggling.

Traveling many routes underground like Harriet Tubman.

Help build a guild of brothers with lyrical skills.

Work out of different fields enhancing my mental shield.

Boarding a battleship that exhibit the will and wits.

Without a ego-trip contemplating my workmanship.

Perhaps I feel fantastic stopping all the dramatics.

Society has a habit to have it go find a magnet.

Air walkers

Shape shifted the beard switched up the cornrows to braids.

Breeze through the blocks hit different roads my escapades.

Challenge my time in a sequence only known to the source.

The only lost is a gain remain framed in a fixed force.

Tower over lower level frequencies with decency.

What's meant for me my memory has a high delivery.

Urgency on the table unstable is erratic allocation.

Bars raising and blazing this occasion tip equations.

Greater than I ever been more polished and shining.

doorways to true findings is blinding to underlining's.

Taste the king words delivered in a future height.

My Atterberry sight move clouds in partial daylight.

off the other

I'm in the door of the hall with my hands on the wall.

Waiting for calls to pour, more of them words that cause.

Reaction of yeah guard keep the right-hand typing.

Bring fever to readers skills is sick when I'm writing.

Touch the masses with literature from a three-name tag.

Never once did I brag contenders lag what I have.

Join a club of spectacular individuals who be working.

Kill a show close the curtain and still be out searching.

We all need to bring in a lifestyle making noise.

Whoever haven't found they joy stuck being coy.

Put a purpose on perspective insight while I'm thinking.

While I'm sinking in the sounds feels as if I been drinking.

Sit this down

Master maneuver who is cooler it's the finalization of what made me what I am in this America.

They cannot hold me my internal is a metamorphosis active never do I practice I'm an estranged Baptist.

Going against whatever wherever however make your bars clever my endeavors wired like Indian summers.

My tantrum in this social media times I draw the line throw up a sign enter a platform Lukewarm I am blind.

Energy kinetic I get it or just forget it remember who said it king is majestic later for methods.

Life on rolled dice which is it keep a juice type associate like blizzard, but I am more like kid wizard.

School of the R push wheels on black tars healed scars war wounds got my style from grant's tomb.

My riverside moment downhill enters a Broadway no melee got to get home and write an essay.

Composition book full of laws by gallotron extend my arms keep a shorty warm and a seed calm.

Doubters heavy haters wanting favors my next chick will not get the Netflix but chill and smoke some good shit.

Evil lurked upon me no injury considers me blue and burgundy favorite colors do not let my eyes see me.

Trilogy of emotion battle bits of contemplation interact with rap doctor prescribed me a high.

Died inside the rise of many vibes coming back is the nineties drive landmark a year hand me a prize.

It's on me

Who else could it be that write bars in twelves?

Without any help these others got some elves.

Type it out no white out it is a one take on the cell phone.

Eight books wrote all alone they wish I left my zone.

Found another way to express my best I take my time control my breath.

Suicidal death on these counterfeits it's a foul mix I rep myself.

Milestone accomplishing stomping into any year I'm in.

Made some friends left associates stuck inside they pad and pen.

Done procrastinating demonstrating working situations.

Some feel it's amazing how I bring forth my creations.

Thankful to the highest for allowing me to become wise.

After my demise I will return behind the sunrise.

"Spirit of Kydd fresh"

Dope fly and cool stepping off and return back.

uneasy mis match here let's secure the latch.

Get me to the issue watch the line missile get you.

Criss cross your riddle sanction all that I been through.

Regulate the gates to the whereabouts and home base.

Don't matter the safe house I home check a state.

Working at a pace to rebuild years of sorrow.

Leave marks of Gallo living for a better tomorrow.

My scenes capture all themes like movie screens.

Budget off my green by any means without extreme.

Filter out distraction take action before something happen.

Avoid crashing while pushing the outer limits and hold caption.

Me lest and dest (remix)

New lines cool rhymes of me, lest and dest.

Nephew to both rewritten to be fresh.

Two guys from different eras that made my life better.

No need to say my name I represent three letters.

JWA THE GUARD king atterberry.

Always forever ready energizer moving steady.

Ciphers built strong great advise on the arm.

So, when I drop multiple verses it's calm before a storm.

Jokers want to laugh until my paragraph address them.

Bars carry hidden lessons holla at BLESS for weapons.

Verbalize the shot with a time check on any clock.

Send a kite to RAP DOC and tell him what I really got.

Sessions I applaud walk on floors that open doors.

Sweat the words out my pores until I empty my core.

Imagery on a flyer exploit the dude who come through.

When you learn from the best just do what you do.

Me lest & dest / Pandemic version

Guess who has returned its the wave runner coming.

Always writing a dozen at a sixteen-bar luncheon.

Punch the world in the grill at face value what's normal.

Out of all that I been through I remain cordial.

Walk around mortal while so many out here awful.

Problems come and go just be mindful and thoughtful.

One man taught me the laws the other bout closing doors.

Together my common cause is to open my pores.

Release the dead side of my ways and pump my brakes.

When it's time to demonstrate I create and dominate.

Through my books I express the best what I profess.

Giving a shout out to my uncles it's me, lest and dest.

You're welcome

Let me break out the cage jump on the wave feeling amazed.

Temperature high blaze so the bar level is raised.

Can I spit it get wicked sporting a button and a fitted?

I'm authentic when you hear it can you feel it in your spirit.

Adapt to sound found underground here I come.

I'm here to have some fun from a place where you begun.

Don't let the nursing scrubs deceive your eyes on my appearance.

It's the apprentice that's relentless dropping lines within a sentence.

Treat the track like a slut never what I'm in the cut.

Can't rush the gentle bust love honeybuns and crush.

Lay my vocals on an instrumental like bodies on a pallet.

Walk around all giddy and high off morning magic.

Addicted to life watch how I pick a beautiful feeling.

No longer am I rearing I am driving with power steering.

Shoot for a section to reside no place to hide.

With the angels versus demons I walk with higher guides.

Invisible rebel

Thinking to myself how to move about the land of lands.

Remove another side of me and come up with master plans.

Design a diagram inside my mind without too much thought.

Change my course speak with the source and build a higher force.

Shield of hope, faith and love to block the ugly hate.

Showing a face creating space where kind people relate.

Witness a doctrine being born around silence and violence.

Form an alliance without bias and dissect the blind science.

Dreams of better days that carry the weight of tomorrow.

Feed the hearts of sorrow with some love in a bottle.

Care for others while you nurture the clearer points of view.

Open the proof expose the truth and see a brighter side of hue.

ALL I KNOW

AS I WALK THIS EARTH THINKING TO MYSELF, HOW DID I REACH THE HEIGHT OF MY LIFE.

I CLOSE MY EYES AND GATHER MY THOUGHTS AND LOOK INTO A MIRROR AND SAY SHEESH YOU ARE WHO YOU ARE AND NOBODY CAN IDENTIFY WHAT YOU HAVE BECOME OR WHAT YOU HAVE ACCOMPLISHED IN RIGHTING YOUR WRONGS AND REMAINING STRONG DURING THE TIME IT TOOK YOU TO GET WHERE YOU HAVE GOTTEN.

FOR SURE ONE THING IS FRIENDS WHICH YOU HAVE GAINED THAT ARE SUPPORTIVE.

FRIENDS THAT YOU HAVE THAT HAVE OPENED THE WINDOW TO THEIR SOUL FOR YOU TO TAKE A LOOK INTO.

THE WORLD IS FILLED WITH UPS AND DOWNS SOMETIMES WE BEAT THE ODDS SOMETIMES WE DONT.

BUT WHEN YOU GIVE A FEW DROPS OF LOVE TO THE ONES THAT HAVE UNCONDITIONAL LOVE FOR YOU MAY IT BE YOUR SPOUSE OR FRIEND OR ASSOCIATE.

YOU GET WHAT YOU RECEIVE AND HOPEFULLY GIVE BACK THROUGH THE SAME MEASURES.

HATRED IS SO HARSH TO MUSTER IN A FRAME OF MENTAL STABILITY.

YOU EITHER SAMPLE THE HATE THATS GIVEN ON A PLATE OF EVIL AWARENESS OR YOU GRAB A DRINK OF PROSPERITY AND JOY AND FEEL REFRESHED.

BLESS THE MOMENT THAT YOU FEEL SO GOOD AND GRASP THE WIND AND REJOICE.

IT WAS ONCE TOLD TO ME BY MY INNER SELF NEVER BECOME A GLORY HOGG IF SOMEONE HAS GOOD COME ABOUT THEM SALUTE THEIR INNER AND OUTER FINDINGS.

BUT FOR THOSE THAT POSSESS THE INTENT TO SELFISHLY DEMEAN OTHERS POWER SOURCE, THAT CARRY THEM ON THE WING OF A BUTTERFLY.

LET THEM DRIFT IN A DEEP ABYSS AND ASK GOD TO FORGIVE THEM AND STILL LOVE THEM AND SHOW THEM THE WORLD.

WE CAN ALWAYS LEARN FROM THE MISTAKES OF OTHERS AND SEE A BRIGHTER DAY WHEN EVER IT IS DISPLAYED ON THE MANTEL OF A CARING SHOW-CASE.

LOVE ON ANOTHER AS A BROTHER OR SISTER IN THE EYES OF GOD WHETHER IT BE BLOOD RELATED KIN, CLOSE KNIT FRIEND OR ENEMY.

LOOK AT ALL THE DEGREES OF BOREDOM, LOOK AT ALL THE DEGREES OF HAPPINESS WAKE UP! WAKE UP! AND LIVE LIFE!!

Left to right it's alright to write

Put it on paper my hand moves across page and speak.

Thoughts come out deep because the center of me leak.

What started off special became commercial to your drama.

Your loyalty wasn't honored so I left and didn't bother.

Signed up for a new detail and worked to where i am.

Keeping a lot of super friends embracing love that's sent.

Heaven side of me disappoint the dark energy.

Sending me down lanes of thought remembering lost memory.

Bright minds think alike on sight capture the image.

Changed out my living where I'm chilling adjusting feelings.

New day arriving cross waves into tomorrow.

Allow my shadow to follow my whole essence
that's modeled.

Live and let live what you get and what you give.

Are the vibes of what you do not what you did be
positive?

So, grow within the world that is globed within our
earth.

Peace to my brothers and sisters and the outer
universe.

Play the airwaves

Let's think about it for a minute place the archive
into music.

Saluting all who do it my influence is the truest.

Aims already deadly I feast on tracks with
medleys.

Break damns capture moments swim outside of
levees.

Picture a caption or a meme assist without a
motive.

This is just a notice I'm focused illuminating
voltage.

Never boxed check parameters outside your
scope.

Speaking tone of folks that know about my
growth.

Is it just your business nah let us distinguish?

Few times I seen this iron lines can kill a Phoenix.

Even after the return never concerned of being
burned.

From what I learned it's my turn to do all things on
my terms.

Play the airwaves verse 2

Bring a elephant mindset to contenders whoever want it.

Throw a jab verbally now you funny in your stomach.

Wondering if the guard really said what he said.

Hell, yeah, I'm standing up while others play in their bed.

Only sleep I'm used to, is the after work special.

Protecting my vessel while your others be in your kennel.

Isn't nothing to spar with the bars I lift the dark.

Knock lines out the park killing lights hitting marks.

Remain sharp with master minds that align with the best.

Never worry about the next so I flex ripping your rep.

If it's a battle of the planet episode call on your G-force.

My power source draw divine laws call up your boss.

never worry

Expression technique when I speak it's unique on top of this beat lay vocals down then it's complete.

Avenues taken no perpetrating while I'm waiting my course of navigating situations in locations.

Cool as fuck break out of ruts with new stuff there's never a bluff, I hold enough with eight in the cut.

Blasphemous bastard want to snake mine I'm inclined toward the divine sending a sign watch how I shine.

Broadcast my frequency without any leniency better have some decency it's KING ATTERBERRY!!

No thrown or kingdom I change my condition within multi dimension swinging until I hit them.

Intro to the outro raining grab your poncho back down your honcho with tornado lines that glow.

Why try and apply never mind I get mines these people must be crazy if you thought I'm blind in your eyes.

My thoughts remain on route without a doubt holding down a house where you at lost in the south.

Write what I might to my delight I strike like workers who refuse to work around poor highlights.

Even kill a starlight with decisions my mission of living bars carry styles of five deadly venoms.

She or he that want to be crazy or messy spin off degrees of Hercules prepare mask for surgery.

Solar roller

Elevation factors what really matter in them dark days.

Shine bright rays against skies that turn grey and stay.

Break codes of the unknown control tone as words reach.

Tread lightly on the meek you can search find and seek.

Miraculous methods no overstepping broad horizons.

Instead of diving just swim to a moment of just arriving.

Justified is the eyes that show lies before the archive.

Lift the veil upon the wise and visualize no compromise.

Tough guy facade exposed by those that know.

Isn't no telling what really show take ropes off the boat.

Got to be underneath and show a method of your chi.

Take a second just to breathe and manifest degrees.

Stick with it

Snatch the janitor kick over his mop bucket and slide off.

Vacation time coming leave the south and head north.

Cop the inexpensive rental for three days on two trips.

Too many heads know my eggshell whip that split.

Gym bag full of autographed books clothes in a backpack.

My son got left back had to work his job, I hear that.

All good my move about ways from here to there.

Call some family on a throw away phone trust under-stairs.

Probably Polly with acquaintances last seen in my twenties.

Eat a small breakfast at Denny's and boycott Wendy's.

Lunch is on the go ate before I reach my destination.

dead location stationed where the church is congregating.

WHAT HECK!!

If it's time to bear arms my short sleeves bear arms.

Hands detonate the bomb to protect me from harm.

Break kneecaps and ankle that try to crush my neck.

Thought the men in blue protect end of the day it's neglect.

Respect who nah the principles are all screwed.

What are my people to do when they come after you?

Can't run from the gun that bust a cap in your back.

Turn on the audio recording that's in the cell phone jack.

Got to have that proof just in case they want you dead.

So, it can go viral and through the net it will spread.

Scary out here in this land they want us all slaved again.

No shackles and chains it's just the old Americans.

Policy

Cats moving funny they hungry acting like weirdos.

Play a brother too close might witness a cyclone.

Temperature uneven on scales masses are covered.

Better duck quick when the words splurge into something.

Attitude in check the mood too cool and smooth.

Distance myself from fools that use the broken rules.

Modesty armed with a writing hand that exhibit.

Extreme thoughts manifested out becoming vicious.

Back trackers of trouble huddle thinking they smart.

Battery operated hearts working by souls' dark.

Candles lit on grounds of where cowards were standing.

Drama unfolds in a cold hole that's abandoned.

Rent peace for moments on life need to be saved.

New waves of ill manners displayed we have to pray.

Shake a hand end violence let's speak to one another.

Somebody family won't have to suffer let's heal our brothers.

Pick up the pieces

Where we from just a place we call home full of love.

Everyday it's just luck when they bust you have to duck.

Get out the reign of terror no umbrella can ever cover.

Why fight against each other death is high in them numbers.

Outside of this covid check the motives of controllers.

Let's stand broad on shoulders of all our past soldiers.

Sad to see exactly what they want in our community.

Within a trilogy of mystery find many ways to breathe.

Been here and there struggle to live is deadly.

Protect your hands and feet besides strengthen your body.

Defend all within children of friends and family.

Grab the world shake it up and maybe rewrite history.

Where to go

Meet the black tad martin still searching for Jenny.

Heard she moved to philly with her young son Benny.

Spoke to Uncle Lenny who got word from brother Kenny.

Last time he saw his daughter she was eating at Denny's.

Running with a crowd from a local neighborhood.

She wore a king atterberry shirt displaying all his books.

Without a physical address this tracker hit the city.

Following different leads hoping the people are friendly.

She left behind essential credentials along with memories.

After her bad relationship threw away her identity.

Lucky for the guardian who had a few connections.

That showed him good expression pointing in the right direction.

Wondering how a woman strong lost faith and hope.

As I got close to the home within the details of the note.

Entered the building climbing stairs inhaling the stagnant air.

For this journey I wasn't prepared to go far and come near.

Knocked on the door a voice spoke who is it what's your name.

I said king and then explained who I was to Jenny Lange.

Elderly woman with grey hair and a cane appeared suddenly.

Resemblance uncanny to my family but looked motherly.

So she asked me inside to have a seat in the kitchen.

There was Jenny at the table sitting as I talked, she listened.

No show

My post on a post never ghost me as a host team shining no joke with a coach from different coast.

The approach is never seared like red meat in metal pans still the man behind the hands discard whatever end.

Turn tables into furniture reconstruct exterior no mike jack in the mirror interior reign superior.

Change the game to pity pat if it's like that not exact here let me retract dismiss a pact roll over crap.

Sitting upon nonsense revive the moment too nappy can't comb it better to disown it without atonement.

Crystal clear is ideas that appear never to fear forever an engineer drive a train to a station that care.

Language altered on the speech when it gets deep and water rise right underneath your feet time is never beat.

Not one for settling perhaps I need the medicine for outsiders that's meddling holistic way better than.

Over the joke my role in the play is advanced where I make moves to enhance the brand while others can't.

Mj the mutiny deep abyss the energy if no longer they are feeling me then I recycle what hide in me.

Allstate

I'm a OG from from a different state with a new face slamming new breaks.

Don't matter the time and day couldn't carry my weight I'm grounding the gate.

Push an all-white in a similar light when I spit bars a gorilla sight.

Darken you're borders you know that I saw ya strike mic like a shark bite.

When they are foolish and ghoulish, I transform ruthless ok my nigga listens to music.

Thing about king no time for a scene bullshit who is this.

Build a buzz around fly traps get zap by the rap I place on this track.

Launch a lyrical attack my poetry packs a wow fact it's back to the raps.

Hip hop head to the fullest degree spitting them words mental telepathy.

Whack ass jokers mean nothing to me armed with a bomb killing your feed.

Poppa doc with the power in hand send a force that jaw crack man.

Won't sound the same your mouth is to blame got a nigga like aww got damn.

Illustration

Indication beyond notation revelation situation banned explanation no creation.

Questions reserved placed on canvas false standards well rounded can't stand it yet still demanded.

Different commandments change laws heavy applause walk through rooms without doors hold up pause.

Unity divided exiled broken emotions accept a token whisper words stolen by those frozen.

Thawed release the flaws of you and yours the cause thoughts soar energy enter pores well absorbed.

Ignite streaks of light with inner sight of nights true delight of getting a taste of peace shine bright.

Visit the past for a laugh return and have a blast finish a draft expose paragraphs fulfill a task.

Heroes and villains' same parents with children wave of feelings many dealings egos never brilliant resilient.

Notice direction accepting lessons without guessing sessions protecting creators blessing with perfection.

Take five

My dreams manifest through the reality of abundance.

Practice oneness, along with those who really want this.

Mindset of those pros that showed a better living.

Hard driven accomplishing missions without tripping.

Only setbacks are traps laid down by off thinking.

Recalibrate initiate the power while your singing.

Heartfelt moments let the tunes brighten your aura.

Uncomfortable heat horror has you searching for sauna.

Back to where you want to be relaxing building energy.

Sharpen up your sensory excuse the blind enemy.

A lot of times the lost can find a line that have them shine.

As we rewind start fresh and exploit ways to grind.

How you feel!

Only gave you a moment to readjust your life.

Biggest sacrifice was nice open the flight site.

Lanes all clear hear the sound in the rain.

Voice drowning in pain mask hurting my brain.

Compromise my breathing barely having air leaking.

Wrote this piece before the weekend my born day creeping.

Enter a Saturday night fever enjoy myself chill mode.

Although the world growing lots of mold inside its soul.

Crack a bottle of good brandy and light something up.

My forty-nine-shine celebrated with a full cup.

Years of manifesting through them true and living sessions.

The gods present lessons dropping jewels no question.

As I project and show my talent just know that it's apparent.

It's **KING ATTERBERRY** the son of **LIL JOE** and **KAREN!**

Brother to the minister of information my blood kin.

Later for these fake friends your third eye closed and.

Holla at the **GUARD** when you wake up real life living.

Just wrote this in my kitchen drinking coffee with intention.

Switch water

left the city in the back of my mind navigate through the world enter a whole different sector building with brothers.

Only thoughts of losing my mother rediscover others what's rougher my steps tougher got to see another.

Plans never divulged carry a titan type mentality no fantasy my reality start grabbing me.

Five fifty-two to exit 0 memorable ride essential deep inside my mental carry high potential.

Backpack with notebook and pens cassette got instrumentals walk-man running sounds through my headphones.

Salt air infiltrate my system cleansing what's polluted i guess this is what my body doing.

Caught a call for employment dressed in black and white apparel, Reeboks on my feet hit the clock as i travel.

nine to five legal deagal land of seagulls and some strange people never know how they treat you when they meet you.

Eye contact handshake off a mistake catch a break slice bread on porcelain plates and eat grapes.

Caution of the officer's code of blue nothing new watch what you do and how you move liars stretch the truth.

Protect the youth let them grow beware of so and so, orb of life looking nice glow is bright enough to hold.

Kiss the air breathe collect your thoughts process environments this lion gets enough hours pass requirements.

Find a way!!

In between the layers of hope, faith, and gratitude.

Move about roam around see the guard in maroon.

Burgundy sweats navy blue sneaks and brand shirt.

They watch my progression inside they heart feeling hurt.

Capital in revenue pick and choose paid my dues.

How I'm going to lose cut loose the goose and join platoons.

Winds of war in front of city corner stores active.

Uniforms in blue storm is masses abusive actions.

Phone cameras and voice recorders live we all matter.

Street professionals' wallets fatter selling Casper.

Old school muscle makes the goons run and tap out.

Snitches fronting hard in your house sitting on couch.

No need to expose already told by the word of mouth.

Might as well get on the road chump and change routes.

New brothers sitting on moments till the money right.

Open the panel check the mantle read the king is nice.

No longer!!

She thought the guard was weak really, I chose not to speak, too much attention off my beak so I shut down my speech.

Now I'm hearing lots of anger it's the stranger that's a danger I'm calling gods rangers to awake her like Sanka.

Words never served as exclusive only inclusive upon her thoughts of what she sought I changed the close course.

Personality of kindness only thing minus the virus on these liars so I disconnect wires and roll like tires.

Perpetual eyes upon a single man who don't have an interest please listen I'm not dissing but we from off dimensions.

Your world and mine is not designed to align my spiritual is lyrical and yours critical dark and miserable.

Find a fix I'm on a list that uplift my given gift don't ever get it twisted I pray to god against anything wicked!

Enjoying times, the here and now is marvelous and wonderful, beautiful, and lovely shine and glow on things ugly!

Gravitate to energy of auras that allow me to explore and adore what I haven't seen before that's allured.

Taste the feelings of new beginnings no endings so I'm bringing the winnings of a great adventure guardian remembering.

So know you're in a good space of all that you want and really searched for, allow my vibes to touch heart mind and core.

Hold on

Bringing it back like old days still use those phrase that gave wave lay where I stay cause its home made.

Played hills with big wheels that made deals with white seals never once did I kneel count bills on windmills.

Dodge singers that tell what's hidden out of your living in the hood it's forbidden yet for cheese cowards listen.

Paint pictures with lines make them shine just for mankind wake up the blind make a sign so they can find.

Crumbs of thought what were sought that was caught for what we fought place strength on the loss, so they gain a full force.

Fly to a stop where I check clock without watch make a sundial with rocks see time change within spots.

Just to be clear I'm only here to bring others near appear without a glare show a pair that join the atmosphere.

Poets unite on this atterberry flight reaching a outer world height keeping and holding our Universal rights.

In time we get better and pull levers on go getters without any pressure gain a treasure while we rock together.

Build a circle of energy the destiny is finally built off high degrees from abilities that's on-stream feeds.

Breeze with company as we see ourselves free open opportunities friendly as our souls be adapting to nature's modesty.

Happiness combined into a good day of peace god bless the connection of the elements inside all of us!

Take one

Reminiscing way back to when I rap from my knapsack listening to tracks, I wore plats under my black cap.

Moves that I made wordplay I gave forever and always placing my thoughts on page introducing a new wave.

From the intro i penciled a few poems to instrumentals end of the day I lent you something cool to hold onto.

Joined ciphers with others steel sharpen steel honing skills bars are concealed just be ready to feel what's revealed.

Mapped out the style and flow from many sounds spent a lot of time around the true and living in my town.

Even movers and shakers givers and takers fake ya searching for a favor mix your flavor before they snake ya.

Hung with runners in my summers in winter with hunters who held hunger during the tundra they mindset was of mum ra.

While them thunder cats was yelling hoooo we saying here we go working for dough still being poor until we found our glow.

Find that what we were looking for holding hammers like mighty THOR his weapon to us metaphor but that life exists no more.

All grown from a young age pick and choose friends in these lion days might end up in a cage that seal fate in dying way.

So when you take heed to the downfalls because the overall is a bad call rise above it and stand tall end of all is a ground floor.

Here again

Walk the neighborhood with my eyes closed
taking steps in loose clothes.

The weather not that hot yet so I'm working out
just to get toned.

Wireless headphones playing tunes list of jams
that hit my mental.

Make my journey and quest real simple free
styling to instrumentals.

Return home and shower get dressed watch the
clock move.

Resume what I was doing before I walked outside
to a sky blue.

Exercise the mind body and soul to control my
vessel image.

Write some poems feel good at home till that
twelfth line is finished.

Thoughts of meals that I make through my skills
as a prep cook.

There's not a thing that I can't make recipes not
overlooked.

Lifestyle style of this Blackman in a world that is
so mixed up.

So people get the part end of the day might just get cut.

Look inside that mirror that show reflection of who you are.

Pray upon your war wounds and god remove the scars.

Rinse away fatigue and then release the old for new.

Better for you is what you do living outside the other you.

Under the sun

Ferry slid across the bay seagulls flying across the salt air.

Following the vessel searching for bits of food everywhere.

Sounds of the water waves splashing on the open bay.

Different life underneath never know what type play.

People out on the deck enjoying what they feel the most.

I guess there's an experience of being on this large boat.

Food and beverage also gift shops with marquee apparel.

Moving at a speed never idle watch both sides of you.

Conversations all around while the ride is sort of bumpy.

Drinks almost spilling while meals fill the hungry.

Movement is still for a few minutes to chill.

Absorb the whole feel until it docks and kill the wheel.

Raise 'em up

Let us all gather around in this time of need please.

We must help raise the people to the highest degree.

Close eyes and meditate place thoughts on bright life.

There are things going on right now let's stand and fight.

Build a community with bridges hang up some quoted pictures.

Our brothers are not niggas and our sisters aren't bitches.

Paint murals on walls that mean so much lifting the youth.

Stop war by martial law end gang violence with a truce.

Have a true understanding bring a meaning to a group.

Tighten up whatever's loose correct the false with a truth.

Never easy but we have to do better and try harder.

Calling all state riders help the problem of survivors.

Not I

Many convos were spoken in a combo of verses.

Let's search where the earth is and get pass the curses.

Find a secret serum, cure all that's been infected.

Wipe the dust off the lessons and maybe the book answer questions.

Divided were the people of an era where I grew up.

Once again hold a cup of good luck peace to king tut.

Call upon my brethren's that keep knowledge better than.

The average that lack status through my presence here's my offering.

Hit the bell as if time were cut short on a game show.

Doing things off the arm with my hand excuse my elbow.

Got to watch the faker takers when are they going to give back.

As I walk on life's tracks, I'm not a well performing act.

Eyeball the poser with a higher conscious motor.

Witness a soldier much older than a dead October.

Back in the central

Don't have the booth catch fire when I spark the mic wires.

What's a beat without an intro all expressed tell your messiah?

Breathe off the sleeve's tracks bleed I'm underneath.

Bring a terror with these bars takeover and try to keep.

Yawl brothers still be playing this is real time finale.

For those who act petty probably because chick caddy.

Place minds in orbit get off it never worth it.

Find a better network to service or build a surface.

The group don't decline in members we just remember.

later for them figures that linger find your September.

Rock steady and hold better choices within this realm.

Knock ops off they mark until we regain the helm.

Line of mine

When I become a giant soon walk with the tyrants.

Witness my deviance when I join the alliance.

My peoples dropping science hearing all that's sincere.

Damn right I appear close and near never to fear.

Bear witness to an atterberry king from southern land.

Surrounded by marsh sand building with sons of man.

Some only get a glance of the real and just be talking.

But frankly when I'm speaking conversations be important.

Play a course on a Tee who be free on lost days.

The guard be on his way you see me post about the bay.

Rise above the bullshit displayed by the mannequin.

My pen is a lightsaber defeating the dark Anakin's.

Possessed by the dark side pull poems out my archive.

They better run and hide cause any moment can be do or die.

I came a long way to being who I have become.

Shining like the sun Harlem world is where I'm from.

Job done

My first book was an intro to the world of writing.

July 2017 hit them with a bolt of lightning.

Then February 2018 caught the penning bug.

Released my second poetry book to show love.

Hands couldn't be still it's the power of the will.

On July second same year showed other how i feel.

No big deal I'm too humble to be a showoff.

When I'm cool, put your coat on as I take mine off.

Joel Harris trilogy of poetry they notice me.

Manifesting all my qualities showing humility.

Blacked out in January 2019.

Released a double bubble for all the poets that have dreams.

We all are special if it's not on the wall in halls.

The King Atterberry edition entered the fall.

One on thanksgiving because they saw my vision.

Another two days before Christmas showed my position.

Now a cousin who I never met before gave me a power.

That I been already acquired so in May I spoke louder.

Medicine tweaked

People already know to the table I bring.

Put yourself in my shoes I'm doing the damn thing.

Never heard to compromise limits pass the sky.

Enter a universe before my demise watch me rise.

Explored Davy Jones locker cleared all my chakras.

My uncle said nephew meet the rap doctor.

Study all the greats that's how I created eight.

Just setting the record straight through the world I navigate.

Continue subject matters expose masked illusions.

Connect with many humans leave those intruding.

Found a corner in the ring as I train with thee estranged.

Let me say what I say and cross lanes on both planes.

While the falsification of information is dissected.

Station myself the truth yes and right I stay protected.

Build a buzz with my cuz and all who rep with us.

So, I never have to rush and discuss what I don't trust.

Hug the love

There is nothing sweeter than feeling your demeanor.

As we lay down listening to sounds between us.

Candles lit natural aroma in the air.

The vibes are alive connective energy everywhere.

Kissing on your aura as my mind explore you.

This is the perfect times to ask you as our minds travel.

Is this from me to you with the marvelous measures of me.

Through my eyes from the sky can be just like candy.

Place my affection between your sensual wanting.

Our warmth can carry the brightness of the sun in the morning.

Refreshing as a cool breeze entering our pleasurable moment.

Here my dear you found a showman that is open.

To whichever expression captured that will remain active.

Allow my physical tactics to assist in your gymnastics.

Touch on your central orchestrate your instrumental.

Open your window as I play with you real gentle.

Who

When I step, I'm in my new shoes searching for my new groove.

Same time she is looking for a boo who make her body move.

Laid back reserve and cool walking like I'm old school.

My old daddy poppa smooth checking woman latitude.

The scent of her perfume sends my thoughts out the jungle.

My inner roar explores the possibilities to cuddle.

That's if all work out right become the brother to her night.

Perhaps wake in the morning to a nice breakfast delight.

So, my conversation will be what is your life expectation.

Right now, what are you facing besides looking amazing.

Planning for a date let's escape world of employment.

Find somewhere nice and quiet to avoid any annoyance.

Speak like a Washington flirt as if I'm atterberry.

Neither one of us will worry about time no need to hurry.

Share a smile upon each other as we search each other's eyes.

This moment fresh and new don't mind if we just improvise.

Element

My last night in housing short visit with family.

Saw elder Nancy and her broke brother Danny.

Quick exchange of convo he still resides on her couch.

Living in the same house moved up north from down south.

Big dawg in the lobby moving nice bags of evergreen.

The young cats copped a few then bounced from the scene.

Gave him a pound and hug mad years his face seen.

Exit out the building while he is building with his team.

Hailed a cab to the Bronx to check my people's baby storm.

Who was hustling with Sean and his loud cousin norm!

Peep them in the park where it's half dark and dim.

Sitting with some friends smoking and drinking counting ends.

As I got close one homie left his post just to peep me.

Called my peoples name out so he would not act unfriendly.

Acknowledgement confirmed so they stopped we walked and talked.

They said peace my brother it's nice to see you here in New York.

Hello!

Looking inside of your world and seeing how you live inside it.

Shows me how amazing and beautiful you are within your inner and outer appearance.

Enjoying time within each other's presence is a highlight of mystery like the universe.

Life around the existence of the unknown illuminating in settings of darkness.

As I explore with my intuition my only vision is to carry out my heart mission.

Sleep with mindfulness of how your rest is wake up sending you my thoughtfulness.

Real men haven't disappeared we are the sun waiting to shine on your forgotten days.

Finding the right time to bring rays of care compassion and true consideration.

Opening the curtain that was closed to the feeling of your not right now moment.

Gradually offering a place for the heart mind and soul to relax chill and be comfortable.

How does one enter the maze of what you figure to be lost and hard to find?

Speak to my undivided attention because I am all ears to what you say and want in your life.

Emergence

Meet a submariner of poetry deep diver of literature.

Expressing with charisma manifest before December.

The wait is well worth it many in this time hurting.

What I notice while observing is the lack of real learning.

Attend meetings with others channel Fredrick Douglass.

Dissect all the stories about Christopher Columbus.

Manual to living what's given halt your speech and just listen.

Only way to come together if we add and kill division.

Connect what's been parted dodge the mark target.

Let's clean up the trash and bag away the garbage.

Unite as a force through the source and use a source.

If the code must be Morse, then mirror back what was lost.

Remember signs and symbols body language from temples.

Everything is simple salute the spoken word generals.

Appreciate the factors of matters that are resolved.

Let The guard king atterberry book you on the card.

location of me

she was searching for the traveler between post on social media.

left in her DM was a poster with three initials that would treat her.

Ticket for her flight on the JWA poetry airline.

checked the gram and Facebook but couldn't find a sign.

so, there it was the instructions what to do with the clues.

little game of peekaboo just to tease her inner issues.

connecting dots found a friend request that matched her direct message.

piecing it all together between the name and the letters.

picture of the king that was in the bottom left corner.

seeds planted in the universe by a meditating farmer.

eye very spiritual with senses of a place not known.

my intergalactic cell phone never roams i stay in
zones.

bring me inside any home my tone change with
frequency.

when they send for me my ability express lots of
humility.

humanitarian handling holding what's golden and
chosen.

mixing potions making lotions rubbing your aura
as it motion.

Hold My Hand!

World changing a lot of minds losing its will too much rust on the wheels that's why our people cannot feel.

What's going on black child where are we now stuck in the clouds nah let it rain remain black and proud.

Absorb kinetic energy from the point of entry galaxy sending me mobility excuse me masking identities.

All I ever wanted for others was to see my tribe of sisters and brothers come from out all that they suffer.

Deep inside the hell hole of anguish and disgust slow down don't even rush I have a backpack full of trust.

Disintegrate the awkward mind state place on your plate band with a group of a chosen few that lift heavy crates.

Tools used acquired assist my roll and stroll while on the road to reaching goals accepting messenger roles.

So my head nod of acceptance in direction of those affected give unity of the cool in me to open opportunity.

Network expand cover lands lend a hand meet and greet different associates form a bond call them your friend.

Life is too short on this plane before I came there was another man behind my own hands that couldn't change.

keep it closed!!

When they keep challenging showing disrespect.

King be off with their neck till he got 'em check.

Isn't nothing set up lines across the air my dear.

Shut down the pattern of steps so they never appear.

Intuition of a spiritual being make sure your eye sees.

Don't be where the art be hanging up with mystery.

Slick as a fox quick as a cat my traps don't latch.

Confusion set in so they mental mind lapse.

Some start tripping and slipping acting different.

One thing they don't listen or really pay attention.

I'm from an alternate place where the conscience lives twice.

Never mixing day and night because my light knows wrong from right.

ADJUSTMENT

Open your chakras walk into tomorrow time is never borrowed write your own gospel.

Strengthen your limitations visit a nation of creation enjoy a great occasion while fixing situations.

Love self-respect what come next is never complex embrace being an architect with poetry after sunset.

Evening vibes come alive while your other side turn and hide create a scribe and let it fly to a platform on the rise.

Absorb feelings in nature while wearing armor of saviors never worry about haters because their energy is glazier.

Lost in a vessel that house a soul that is cold and out of control that their mind is sold to a darkness untold.

Carrying a sword from legionaries who shine bright light up the night with a glow that ignite your inner sight.

What's visible in front view can be misconstrued and ridiculed mix the old and new just present it on cue.

Bypass the premises with brilliance and deliverance my appearance carry diligence without any resilience.

Appetite for knowledge cross boundaries of discovery there is nothing like loving the better of side me.

Living condition

Some fathers don't bother I am my son permanent marker.

Dudes don't challenge her might switch coast to dodger.

Flight to Los Angeles special drinks legal cannabis.

Hit the food truck in Long Beach enjoy the sandwiches.

Never one to entertain games when love is strained.

Whatever I overcame tornado the hurricanes.

Channel my afternoons with yesterday's tomorrow.

Gift people with combos it's the sorrow of my shadow.

She exploits a high interest the king doesn't want to hear it.

Only a goddess to the guardian can open his spirit.

Move around in Stacey Adams slick shirt and dapper pants.

Got to call to change it all hit New York on a chance.

Drive around location until I reach my destination.

Grabbed a few books on celebrating through elevation.

So, I leave behind the trees and the smell from restaurants.

As I park enjoy my coffee with an egg and cheese croissant.

Living condition pt.2

Thought some were thankful more like ungrateful.

In life they won't face you halfway they played you.

Intentions measured but not really by a long shot.

No longer give you time break the clock and the watch.

Wrist free the one eighty delivery was part you and me.

Take the drive out the PC now let's check your telepathy.

Obituaries and eulogies that history is far gone.

The poems can turn to songs book of joel read the psalm.

Back turned you just learned dumb shit that got urned.

Burned in a different world where no one is concerned.

Duality of duties keep levels peaked while the meter blink.

Can't think heart sink don't save the last dance make it a drink.

Crash till the morning good greeting hit your phone.

Whatever is left alone it's never spoke on phantom zoned.

Lift a voice as people know now what has become damaged.

Its apparent conversation is not in the same language.

Where they go!

They want the voucher to success why do some minds think less.

Many methods to process understand your own process.

Find portals that's normal be cordial who saw you.

For those who are thoughtful may just be resourceful.

Hands that be extended without a favor mentioned.

Moves made with intention create waves of living.

Inside be guided outside be reminded.

Never allow your spirit to be divided with climates.

Senses of remembrance captured on a pretense.

Synchronized sequence evolutionary defense.

Unborn natural, letters found in a capsule.

Inscribed by a jackal suggestive thinking of a chaplain.

Keepers of the shield secure and storage meals.

Prepare a platter of raw data encrypted with a seal.

Nothing manufactured only chaptered and page numbered.

Have a seat, come and eat, fill your mind if it hungers.

Open sesame pt.5

Soon we search through the rubble building blocks have crumbled.

These are days of the devil society is in deep trouble.

My wings of prayer travel through hell and come out a balanced scale.

Mask of illusion is being worn face that you see is hidden well.

Demonic company presidents and they dark hearted army.

Treat some of their good employees as if they are working in a safari.

It's a journey getting work done mentally what's your outcome.

Hold your head never be fearsome of the evil on the interim.

Then again some don't check modern enslavement we are trapped in.

The guardian sees what's happening, so I focus on channeling.

Through practicing and managing won't see the guard panicking.

Exercising while battling dismantling all that they are sanctioning.

Questioning what they verbalize advertisements of suicide.

Reading between the lies close my lids and open third eye.

Who sleeping who peeking I am with a team that's truth seeking?

My weekends be breathing off the five days my feet screaming.

How 'bout a dozen!!

I stand in line with the peasants the hungry and non-gifted.

Soon as a cheek is turned raise a session minds lifted.

Grab a handful of brothers set forth on a journey.

Mission time is early leave south Jersey with no worry.

Ancestral mentality other side of me is magically.

Whatever i form manually is built to full capacity.

Sacred lessons of stillness inside a meditated mind.

If I'm blind produce a shine that ignite lines in designs.

Diagrams of maps move a vessel pass the traps.

Even the strongest nets won't catch the guard who came back.

Disguised to assist fellow brothers to escape.

One of the greatest faces of hate losing dignity, pride, and faith.

Tag along if your reborn bare feet the earth on different grounds.

Hid my invisible crown in towns wherever I hear absent sounds.

All the whispers in the air that appear to open ears.

I hear through the creator also I see through sunny tears.

Two lovers

Thought it was you and I just forget the other guy

Allow my eyes to look inside while your heart is open wide.

Provide you with mystery and replay our history.

Remember kissing me as I caressed your body.

Touch on moments where there were no dark days.

All the times you were afraid I moved them all away.

While your smile was kept beautiful instead of miserable.

As we walked around, I saw different men hitting on you.

Only by a stare and a look I moved you closer.

When your girlfriends had you doubt, I rebuilt my motor.

Ran with an exquisite living purpose of being.

Brought to life your dreaming yet they had you scheming.

So, I turned into a soldier of love and found another.

Who could open a window and look inside her lover?

No longer on standby I rise like no other, bye!

Wipe the tears from your eyes we gave it a good try.

Cross the line

To be so in love with you and always so comfortable.

Amazing and wonderful that you allowed me to know you.

Our worlds are so personal can't ever stop thinking bout.

The time I'm in my house on my couch I'm in a drought.

So, I pray maybe one day you receive my special May Day.

Send a signal to the shore I reside in north cape May.

Waiting for that beacon of light to shine upon me.

Meet you at a destination with my angels' army.

Music and love are so well combined.

As if affection and intimacy bring forth sunny weather.

Good vibes and prosperity of existing in great moments.

This is my open letter written by me the chosen poet.

Gotta get right

About a week ago Larry got shot between two
cars.

Pushing his lady shopping cart at the local
Walmart.

Nay Sayers stated that the beef was over side
chicks.

Should have said bye chick and placed her with
his sidekick.

Laying up now inside the hospital with nurses.

Doctors diagnosed him while he is yelling out with
curses.

Street stories mixed up different tales of realness.

Many know the killers who work for drug dealers.

Abdul-Haleem salaam from out state know all
parties.

Trying to squash the issue that's involving many
bodies.

Kaleidoscope of thoughts running through his
lucid mind.

Trying to figure out who lying and who was spying
on the line.

Men in blue appeared at his room door flashing their badge.

Speaking about a suspect that they bagged inside a cab.

Hidden camera caught snapping a shot time to identify.

Amnesia set in familiar face was his alibi.

It's your boy

Leave my mark on whatever I touch pushing the limits.

Formulator of words enter a sentence mail my pendant.

Three initials that I go by air line a verse to track.

Only reason claim I'm whack because I am an artifact.

Peep the odds on that scratch your dirty dingy raps.

House your bars in a trap against the ropes don't believe that.

Unseen for many years how I appear to here and now.

Got an unnatural flow mixed with an abstract new style.

Grab energy from a full moon and manifest something new.

Grand rising upon a morning practicing till afternoon.

Pen game estranged I'm sick from music beating me.

Live and die resurrect watch them haters become fidgety.

Get your love

Do not wait on what is already available to your heart.

Make a move and begin to embark on a fresh start.

Leave alone what is old and enjoy a story untold.

Experience a warmth that is rich like pieces of gold.

Something so hypnotic that also can be erotic.

So healthy pass platonic passion has some of this tonic.

Purified and extracted strengthened with curious magic.

Wear a aura under your fabric feel the care on all that matters.

Look into a world that has reopened with evolution.

Where energy is not polluted and ruined only blessed with music.

Melodic and carefree kiss the air that you have and breathe.

Amazing what you have when god send to you a newer me.

Open the door

Walking through the eras as my mind drift and recognize.

Applications of self that is applied through the other side.

Place prayers in the air as I kneel and speak and whisper.

Anything that differ perhaps trigger all that's remembered.

Search inside the years and months peep the days of memory.

End of time let it be, magnify the loss with Hennessy.

Adapt to change feel the pain allow the eyes to spill tears.

Hurt appear and disappear enjoy the moment that I'm here.

Walk into the building of knowing where I'm going.

Laugh while I'm joking happiness cannot be broken.

Test the wheels of fate as it turns remain in my two.

Only do what you do because the greater times are due.

To the Queens

My dedication to you queens who move around in different scenes.

Appreciating what you bring by many means a lot of things.

Strong woman holding Court within your pure righteous state.

As a king I see your face and how you love to demonstrate.

Beautiful and sexy nothing un-pretty and ugly.

Conducting yourself lovely even humorous and funny.

Grounded by the bases of your heart, mind, and soul.

Knowing what you know, keeping control while on the go.

Adapt to environments where the world can be cold.

Precious women never fold you fought too hard to reach your goal.

Facing challenges of the sexes within society solar plexus.

After working so hard please know where your rest is.

Make a day

Way above minimal never look pitiful always been original 45s are critical.

Born again lyrical weekends be special never will I test you only bless you when I catch you.

Arm strong sort of long stocky with spiritual armor.

Anytime a bomber to a track or acapella stormer.

Heat up like a sauna spit them poems as if I warned ya.

Change my style to any form of New York or California.

Mainstream when I change teams playing with dough makers.

Movers and shakers elevate on elevators get the paper.

Then in comes your boy who signature many things.

With the proper backing probably reload the king.

Ching Ching change is always good turned into bills.

Without fatigue I can breathe going up and down hills.

And chill isn't nothing to the science on the build.

You can see it in my grill I represent how i feel.

It's right there!

When I change states my third eye switch to demographics.

My habit spread magic those who want it they can have it.

Elaborate practice well-crafted mood is Jurassic.

Open my mind with stillness I'm manual and automatic.

From something new and fresh absorb it into your flesh.

One day I'll do a show while visiting the west.

Some become stuck inside a hut full of so what.

Cuffed inside a bluff still playing with candy crush.

Kick rocks and move dust lines are long shoulders touch.

My hands float across board while other nice with brush.

MR.JWA go places regardless of covid cases.

When I leave its small traces placing my foot on amazement.

Respect the loyalty

My back turned memories gone disable my concern.

Lesson learned from getting burned how about you take a turn.

Move along writing poem only hand typing me.

Keep my company outside of house I just let it be.

Settle for less I suggest my eyes closed I profess.

Second guess nah I show the world how I manifest.

What I do while in the mood side of me very cool.

Do not have a point to prove only show how I move.

Difference is better biz exploit my gift that's positive.

Climb the ladder reach the top without asking for a lift.

Love shown heartily felt return a favor to a friend.

Nobody loses anything together it's a win-win.

Razzle dazzle!

It's the return of the shadow from out the dark dim lighting.

Excuse the new sighting thunderstorms keep me writing.

I emerge from out the rain through a bright lightning portal.

Despite my code of ethics, I'm half immortal when I'm cordial.

Put my stamp along with others enter areas of discussion.

Better watch who you are trusting might interrupt your hustling.

Believe in the here and now I embrace the hug and pound.

Remain on solid ground where my peace is lower sounds.

Giving my all is like a chore that I remember as a kid.

All I do is try to give and live and stay positive.

Once told to me by the god was move accordingly.

So I connect and walk a path truly yours with my poetry.

Humble on the mission discard crazy attention.

When the soul is spiritually driven, I stop look and listen.

Intuition of a messenger that carry notes in life.

I just really begun to raise the bar of living right.

Check out the Let's Talk group on Facebook, Let's Talk Poetry Corner on YouTube, or my Instagram about the show!

IG: King_atterberry7 & mentallity9

All books available on amazon!

Search under the titles.

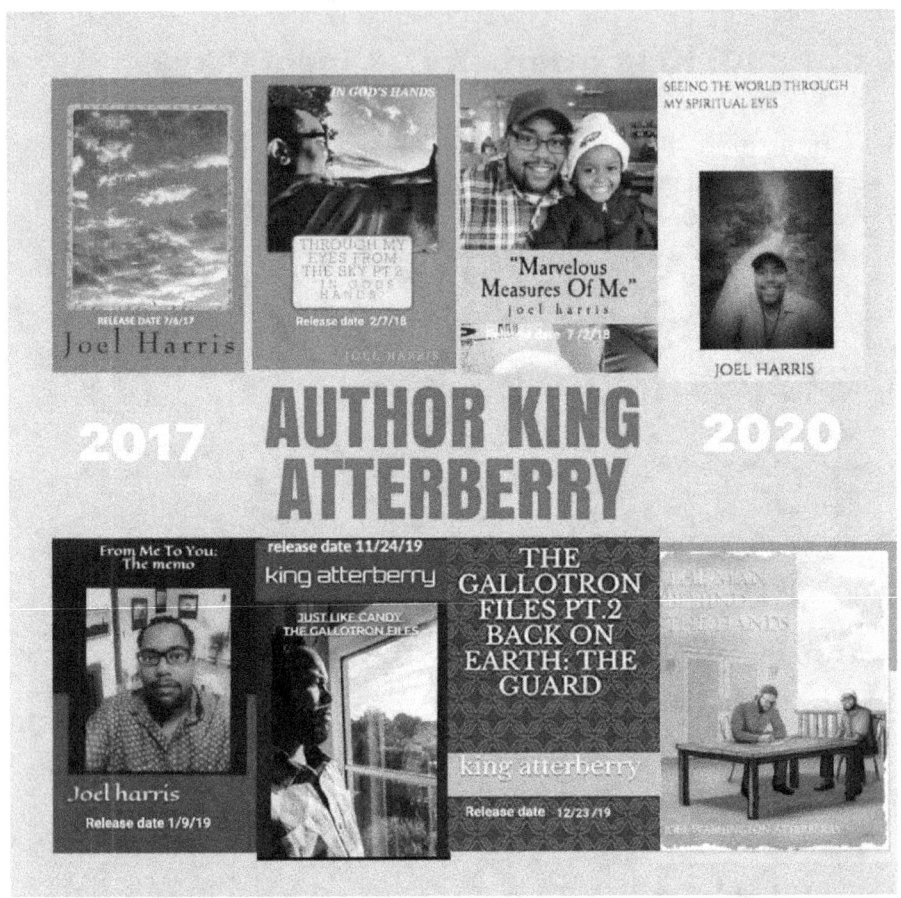

Through My Eyes from the Sky
Through My Eyes from the Sky, Part 2
Marvelous Measures of Me
Seeing the World Through My Spiritual Eyes
From Me to You: The Memo". January 2019
Just Like Candy: The Gallotron Files
The Gallotron Files, Part 2. Back on Earth
The Man Behind the Hands

My sample

of

all eight books of poetry

Mr. Joel Washington Atterberry